first name
 last name
Age
Sex
Country
City

What do you do in life

Your message to the world

first name
 last name
Age
Sex
Country
City

What do you do in life

Your message to the world

This tutorial is for creating new friendships with friends from all over the world in order to exchange knowledge between you and expand the environment of friendship. The idea of this diary is to establish a friendship with different countries remotely via social media and send this mentor to him in order to write something about the world and then ask him to send it to a friend in another country and this one after another until you reach the last person and He returns it to you.

first name
 last name
Age
Sex
Country
City

What do you do in life

Your message to the world

first name
 last name
Age
Sex
Country
City

What do you do in life

Your message to the world

first name
 last name
Age
Sex
Country
City

What do you do in life

Your message to the world

first name
 last name
Age
Sex
Country
City

What do you do in life

Your message to the world

first name
 last name
Age
Sex
Country
City

What do you do in life

Your message to the world

first name
 last name
Age
Sex
Country
City

What do you do in life

Your message to the world

first name
 last name
Age
Sex
Country
City

What do you do in life

Your message to the world

first name
 last name
Age
Sex
Country
City

What do you do in life

Your message to the world

first name
 last name
Age
Sex
Country
City

What do you do in life

Your message to the world

first name
 last name
Age
Sex
Country
City

What do you do in life

Your message to the world

first name
 last name
Age
Sex
Country
City

What do you do in life

Your message to the world

first name
 last name
Age
Sex
Country
City

What do you do in life

Your message to the world

first name
 last name
Age
Sex
Country
City

What do you do in life

Your message to the world

first name
 last name
Age
Sex
Country
City

What do you do in life

Your message to the world

first name
 last name
Age
Sex
Country
City

What do you do in life

Your message to the world

first name
 last name
Age
Sex
Country
City

What do you do in life

Your message to the world

first name
 last name
Age
Sex
Country
City

What do you do in life

Your message to the world

first name
 last name
Age
Sex
Country
City

What do you do in life

Your message to the world

first name
 last name
Age
Sex
Country
City

What do you do in life

Your message to the world

first name
 last name
Age
Sex
Country
City

What do you do in life

Your message to the world

first name
 last name
Age
Sex
Country
City

What do you do in life

Your message to the world

first name
 last name
Age
Sex
Country
City

What do you do in life

Your message to the world

first name
 last name
Age
Sex
Country
City

What do you do in life

Your message to the world

first name
 last name
Age
Sex
Country
City

What do you do in life

Your message to the world

first name
 last name
Age
Sex
Country
City

What do you do in life

Your message to the world

first name
 last name
Age
Sex
Country
City

What do you do in life

Your message to the world

first name
 last name
Age
Sex
Country
City

What do you do in life

Your message to the world

first name
 last name
Age
Sex
Country
City

What do you do in life

Your message to the world

first name
 last name
Age
Sex
Country
City

What do you do in life

Your message to the world

first name
 last name
Age
Sex
Country
City

What do you do in life

Your message to the world

first name
 last name
Age
Sex
Country
City

What do you do in life

Your message to the world

first name
 last name
Age
Sex
Country
City

What do you do in life

Your message to the world

first name
last name
Age
Sex
Country
City

What do you do in life

Your message to the world

first name
 last name
Age
Sex
Country
City

What do you do in life

Your message to the world

first name
 last name
Age
Sex
Country
City

What do you do in life

Your message to the world

first name
 last name
Age
Sex
Country
City

What do you do in life

Your message to the world

first name
 last name
Age
Sex
Country
City

What do you do in life

Your message to the world

first name
 last name
Age
Sex
Country
City

What do you do in life

Your message to the world

first name
 last name
Age
Sex
Country
City

What do you do in life

Your message to the world

first name
 last name
Age
Sex
Country
City

What do you do in life

Your message to the world

first name
 last name
Age
Sex
Country
City

What do you do in life

Your message to the world

first name
 last name
Age
Sex
Country
City

What do you do in life

Your message to the world

first name
 last name
Age
Sex
Country
City

What do you do in life

Your message to the world

first name
 last name
Age
Sex
Country
City

What do you do in life

Your message to the world

first name
 last name
Age
Sex
Country
City

What do you do in life

Your message to the world

first name
 last name
Age
Sex
Country
City

What do you do in life

Your message to the world

first name
 last name
Age
Sex
Country
City

What do you do in life

Your message to the world

first name
 last name
Age
Sex
Country
City

What do you do in life

Your message to the world

first name
 last name
Age
Sex
Country
City

What do you do in life

Your message to the world

first name
 last name
Age
Sex
Country
City

What do you do in life

Your message to the world

first name
 last name
Age
Sex
Country
City

What do you do in life

Your message to the world

first name
 last name
Age
Sex
Country
City

What do you do in life

Your message to the world

first name
 last name
Age
Sex
Country
City

What do you do in life

Your message to the world

first name
 last name
Age
Sex
Country
City

What do you do in life

Your message to the world

first name
 last name
Age
Sex
Country
City

What do you do in life

Your message to the world

first name
 last name
Age
Sex
Country
City

What do you do in life

Your message to the world

first name
 last name
Age
Sex
Country
City

What do you do in life

Your message to the world

first name
 last name
Age
Sex
Country
City

What do you do in life

Your message to the world

first name
 last name
Age
Sex
Country
City

What do you do in life

Your message to the world

first name
 last name
Age
Sex
Country
City

What do you do in life

Your message to the world

first name
 last name
Age
Sex
Country
City

What do you do in life

Your message to the world

first name
 last name
Age
Sex
Country
City

What do you do in life

Your message to the world

first name
 last name
Age
Sex
Country
City

What do you do in life

Your message to the world

first name
 last name
Age
Sex
Country
City

What do you do in life

Your message to the world

first name
 last name
Age
Sex
Country
City

What do you do in life

Your message to the world

first name
 last name
Age
Sex
Country
City

What do you do in life

Your message to the world

first name
 last name
Age
Sex
Country
City

What do you do in life

Your message to the world

first name
 last name
Age
Sex
Country
City

What do you do in life

Your message to the world

first name
 last name
Age
Sex
Country
City

What do you do in life

Your message to the world

first name
 last name
Age
Sex
Country
City

What do you do in life

Your message to the world

first name
 last name
Age
Sex
Country
City

What do you do in life

Your message to the world

first name
 last name
Age
Sex
Country
City

What do you do in life

Your message to the world

first name
 last name
Age
Sex
Country
City

What do you do in life

Your message to the world

first name
 last name
Age
Sex
Country
City

What do you do in life

Your message to the world

first name
 last name
Age
Sex
Country
City

What do you do in life

Your message to the world

first name
 last name
Age
Sex
Country
City

What do you do in life

Your message to the world

first name
 last name
Age
Sex
Country
City

What do you do in life

Your message to the world

first name
 last name
Age
Sex
Country
City

What do you do in life

Your message to the world

first name
 last name
Age
Sex
Country
City

What do you do in life

Your message to the world

first name
 last name
Age
Sex
Country
City

What do you do in life

Your message to the world

first name
 last name
Age
Sex
Country
City

What do you do in life

Your message to the world

first name
last name
Age
Sex
Country
City

What do you do in life

Your message to the world

first name
 last name
Age
Sex
Country
City

What do you do in life

Your message to the world

first name
 last name
Age
Sex
Country
City

What do you do in life

Your message to the world

first name
 last name
Age
Sex
Country
City

What do you do in life

Your message to the world

first name
 last name
Age
Sex
Country
City

What do you do in life

Your message to the world

first name
 last name
Age
Sex
Country
City

What do you do in life

Your message to the world

first name
 last name
Age
Sex
Country
City

What do you do in life

Your message to the world

first name
 last name
Age
Sex
Country
City

What do you do in life

Your message to the world

first name
 last name
Age
Sex
Country
City

What do you do in life

Your message to the world

first name
 last name
Age
Sex
Country
City

What do you do in life

Your message to the world

first name
 last name
Age
Sex
Country
City

What do you do in life

Your message to the world

first name
 last name
Age
Sex
Country
City

What do you do in life

Your message to the world

first name
 last name
Age
Sex
Country
City

What do you do in life

Your message to the world

first name
 last name
Age
Sex
Country
City

What do you do in life

Your message to the world

first name
 last name
Age
Sex
Country
City

What do you do in life

Your message to the world

Please the last person to fill out the last page of the memo, return the book to the first person who wrote it because it his book , and you can also do the same.

All people signatures

thank you